Navigating Certification

What Works!

What Works! is a series of books written by Bobbie Faulkner that will help teachers prepare for National Board Certification and beyond.

Other Books by Bobbie Faulkner

Successful Strategies for Pursuing National Board Certification (2011)

Successful Strategies for Middle Childhood Generalists Pursuing National Board Certification (2012)

Successful Writing Strategies for National Board Certification (2014)

Successful Strategies for Pursuing National Board Certification: Version 3.0, Components 1 and 2 (2015)

Successful Strategies for Pursuing National Board Certification: Version 3.0, Components 3 and 4 (2016)

Navigating Certification

Success with the National Board for Professional Teaching Standards Process for Maintenance of Certification

Bobbie Faulkner

ROWMAN & LITTLEFIELD
Lanham • Boulder • New York • London

Published by Rowman & Littlefield
An imprint of The Rowman & Littlefield Publishing Group, Inc.
4501 Forbes Boulevard, Suite 200, Lanham, Maryland 20706
www.rowman.com

6 Tinworth Street, London SE11 5AL, United Kingdom

British Library Cataloguing in Publication Information Available

Library of Congress Cataloging-in-Publication Data

Names: Faulkner, Bobbie, 1947– author.
Title: Navigating certification : success with the National Board for Professional Teaching Standards process for maintenance of certification / Bobbie Faulkner.
Description: Lanham, Maryland : Rowman & Littlefield, 2021. | Series: What works! | Summary: "Navigating Certification takes the candidate through the stages, beginning to end, of this new Maintenance of Certificate process"— Provided by publisher.
Identifiers: LCCN 2020048591 (print) | LCCN 2020048592 (ebook) | ISBN 9781475858501 (paperback) | ISBN 9781475858518 (ebook)
Subjects: LCSH: Teachers—Certification—United States. | Teaching—Standards—United States. | National Board for Professional Teaching Standards (U.S.)
Classification: LCC LB1771 .F364 2021 (print) | LCC LB1771 (ebook) | DDC 371.1—dc23
LC record available at https://lccn.loc.gov/2020048591
LC ebook record available at https://lccn.loc.gov/2020048592

Contents

Preface

The National Board for Professional Teaching Standards (NBPTS) process for Maintenance of Certification (MOC) is designed based on best practices and teacher feedback to ensure that Board Certified Teachers continue to grow professionally while maintaining a strong impact on student learning. The MOC process begins with the 2020–2021 cycle, becoming the new pathway for National Board Certified Teachers (NBCTs) to maintain their certification.

You have already demonstrated that you are an accomplished teacher. The MOC measures how you have continued to grow in your professional experiences. It provides evidence that your teaching practice still exemplifies the Five Core Propositions, the Standards for your certificate area, and the Architecture of Accomplished Teaching.

Acknowledgments

I'd like to acknowledge those who have encouraged me to continue growing and learning. First, going back in time, Nancy Gallagher Creighton, former director of Scottsdale's Career Ladder Program, whose open mind and leadership allowed National Board Certification take root in the Scottsdale Unified School District.

Dr. Kathy Wiebke and the wonderful staff at the Arizona K–12 Center have been visionary in their support of National Board Certification candidates in all phases of the National Board process. They have financially, emotionally, and academically supported teachers certifying for the first time, those renewing their certificate, and those now completing the MOC process.

Last, but not least, my Scottsdale Cohort sisters—Susan Leonard, Mary Zongolowicz, Abbey Bobbett, and Tammy Andreas—who encouraged me at every step, every bridge I've crossed to reach this point. They are Candidate Support Providers for all National Board Candidates in Scottsdale, including those beginning the MOC process.

Introduction

Navigating Certification: Success with the National Board for Professional Teaching Standards Process for Maintenance of Certification is the next step in the *What Works!* book series for first-time National Board Candidates. Two books in that series are available for initial certification. This book is written specifically for National Board Certified Teachers (NBCTs) who are ready to begin the new Maintenance of Certification (MOC) process.

Navigating Certification is not endorsed by the National Board for Professional Teaching Standards (NBPTS), or any other entity. This book is the result of my many years of personal experiences as a Candidate Support Provider and coach with first-time and renewal candidates. It is not meant to be a "CliffsNotes" type of publication one can use to circumvent the official NBPTS Instructions. The MOC Instructions from the National Board are the paramount/ultimate resource.

Navigating Certification contains information, interpretations, tips, and examples created solely for the purposes of illustration and are not endorsed by the NBPTS. Keep the following in mind:

- The author is not a trained assessor and does not imply that any samples, tips, or scenarios in the book would lead to a favorable decision in the MOC process.
- All samples are hypothetical and fabricated, not from actual candidate work.
- *Navigating Certification* is as current as I could possibly make it. As time passes, the NBPTS occasionally updates instructions, so it is the responsibility of the candidate to be sure to use only the *current* version of the Maintenance of Certification Instructions found on the National Board website (https://www.nbpts.org/national-board-certification/maintenance-of-certification/).

Navigating Certification: Success with the National Board for Professional Teaching Standards Process for Maintenance of Certification is a labor of love. It is my hope that using this resource will make your MOC journey just a little easier, more meaningful, and successful.

Chapter One

What Is Maintenance of Certification?

MOC BACKGROUND

The Maintenance of Certification (MOC) is designed to recognize National Board Certified Teachers (NBCTs) who continue to grow professionally and maintain a positive impact on student learning. The MOC process continues to rely on the foundational documents that are the backbone of the National Board Certification process, namely the Five Core Propositions, the National Board certificate-specific Standards, and the Architecture of Accomplished Teaching (AAT). Meeting the MOC requirements extends a Board Certified Teacher's certification for five more years and has replaced the former renewal process. The MOC is the National Board's response to calls from states to more closely align the National Board Certification process with their state licensure renewal practices. This will allow states to permit National Board Certification to become a "fast track" to state licensure renewal, waiving requirements for teachers who earn and maintain an active NBPTS certificate.

THE FIVE CORE PROPOSITIONS

When you were originally certified, you studied the Five Core Propositions, which are the heart of the National Board process. The Propositions outline the expectations and values for what accomplished teachers should know and be able to do. They are the umbrella under which the other elements of the National Board Certification process are organized and are foundational in the MOC process as well. The Propositions describe accomplishment in the following areas:

- *Proposition 1: Teachers are committed to students and their learning.* Accomplished teachers know the developmental levels of their students, believe all students can learn regardless of background, and use their knowledge to design effective instruction for all students.
- *Proposition 2: Teachers know the subjects they teach and how to teach those subjects to students.* Building upon their knowledge of students, accomplished teachers advance their own understanding of their content area and develop a wide range of strategies to set high and worthwhile goals to teach that subject matter to their students.
- *Proposition 3: Teachers are responsible for managing and monitoring student learning.* Accomplished teachers know how to manage, motivate, monitor, and assess student learning by planning appropriate learning sequences to achieve the desired outcomes and adjusting instruction as needed. Accomplished teachers also know how to structure the learning environment for optimum learning.
- *Proposition 4: Teachers think systematically about their practice and learn from experience.* Accomplished teachers analyze student learning and reflect on their teaching practice. They then determine the next set of high and worthwhile goals, implement instruction, and continue the analysis and reflection cycle.

- *Proposition 5: Teachers are members of learning communities.* Accomplished teachers collaborate with other professionals, parents, and their larger community to support and enhance student learning.

THE NATIONAL BOARD STANDARDS

Each certificate area contains a set of National Board Teaching Standards. These Standards identify specific knowledge, skills, and attitudes that support accomplished practice while emphasizing the holistic nature of teaching. They identify how a teacher's professional judgment is reflected in action and how they reflect the Five Core Propositions. These are the Standards you showed were embedded in your practice when you originally certified, and they continue to be used in the MOC process. It may have been a while since you actively read the Five Core Propositions and the Standards for your certificate area, so I recommend a thorough rereading as you prepare for the MOC process.

THE ARCHITECTURE OF ACCOMPLISHED TEACHING

The Architecture of Accomplished Teaching is the National Board version of an accomplished lesson plan. It is presented in the helix graphic found in the General Portfolio Instructions and also within the "MOC Instructions" document (https://www.nbpts.org/wp-content/uploads/MOC_Instructions.pdf). The helix contains six steps and each step is connected to one or more of the Core Propositions. Here they are in a nutshell.

Step 1: Know Your Students (Proposition 1)

- Who are they? Where are they *now* in their learning? Where should you begin?

- How do you incorporate this knowledge into your lesson planning?

Step 2: Set High and Worthwhile Goals (Proposition 1)

- How do your goals connect with your National Board Standards and component instructions?
- What knowledge about your students influences the goals you set?
- What do you want your students to know at the end of the lesson or unit?

Step 3: Implement Instruction (Proposition 2)

- What approaches do you plan to use to accomplish your goals?
- In what sequence might you plan the strategies you plan to use?
- How will the strategies support your students' learning?
- What is your rationale for implementing instruction this way?
- What criteria might you use to decide if and/or when to use another strategy?

Step 4: Evaluate Student Learning (Proposition 3)

- How will you assess student learning?
- Why did you choose these methods, for these students, at this time, in this setting?
- What will success for your students look like?
- What evidence will let you know if the instruction was successful—or not?
- What, if anything, did the assessment(s) tell you about your instruction?
- What are next steps?

Step 5: Reflect on the Effectiveness of Your Lesson Design and Decisions (Proposition 4)

- How do you know if you made the right choices?
- What was successful and what was not?
- How could students reflect on their own learning?

Step 6: Set New, High, Worthwhile Goals (Proposition 3)

- How will you know it is time to move on in the lesson/unit sequence?
- What indicators will you use to set new goals?

An acronym to help you remember the steps is SSTARS:

- **S**tudents: Know your students and how they learn.
- **S**et high, worthwhile, appropriate goals.
- **T**each using appropriate, effective strategies.
- **A**ssess student learning using a variety of evaluation types and formats.
- **R**eflect on your teaching and students' progress.
- **S**tart the process again.

The use of the AAT is less prominent in the MOC process than it was when you originally certified, but it is embedded within some prompts—so do review it as you work.

THE SCORING RUBRIC

The MOC process is scored holistically. You will not receive a numerical score like you did when you were originally certified. You will either maintain your certification or you will not. However, the degree to which you meet the rubric criteria plays a major role in determining whether you have presented sufficient evidence of accomplished teaching. I will delve into more specifics in a later chapter. Just know that studying the Evaluation Rubric can impact the quality of the work you submit.

MOC AT A GLANCE/OVERVIEW

The MOC process consists of a portfolio made up of *two* interrelated components. These components draw upon *two* Professional Growth Experiences (PGEs), *both related to your original certificate and developmental area.*

- Component 1 will focus on the two PGEs you choose to represent your professional growth since your original certification. You'll choose *one* of the PGEs to be used for/applied to your certificate-specific video lesson for Component 2.
- Component 2 is directly connected to one of the PGEs from Component 1. You'll demonstrate its application in a video with a group of students within the developmental level and content area of your original certification area.

Overall, the MOC submission must demonstrate that your professional growth continues to align with the Five Core Propositions, the National Board Standards, and the Architecture of Accomplished Teaching in your certificate area.

The MOC process is based on parts of the Profile of Professional Growth in the previous renewal process that asked NBCTs to demonstrate that their practices are consistent with the high standards National Board Certification represents. However, because the certification period is for a shorter length of time than the original renewal process, the MOC process has been streamlined and now has two parts compared to the Profile of Professional Growth, which had four parts.

MOC FACTS AND FICTION

FICTION: MOC costs the same as the original renewal process: $1275.
FACT: MOC is much less expensive, costing $495 plus a $75 registration fee as of this writing.

FICTION: The amount of work is similar to the original certification process and/or the former renewal process.
FACT: Candidates who participated in the MOC pilot study reported an average of 53 hours of work time, which is about half the time required by the former renewal process and much less than the 200+ hours logged for their original certification.

FICTION: The MOC process will be extraordinarily rigorous.
FACT: Nine in ten NBCTs who attempted the former renewal process were successful. Similar statistics are expected with the MOC process.

FICTION: The MOC process experience will be as intense as the initial certification process.
FACT: MOC is not the same as repeating the initial certification process. You have already established that you are an accomplished teacher. The MOC process establishes that you have *maintained* your status as an accomplished teacher. You are not starting over.

FICTION: Teachers can't complete MOC if they aren't currently a classroom teacher or if they are teaching in an area different from their initial certification.
FACT: NBCTs who don't currently teach students or now teach in an area different from their initial certification are eligible to complete MOC. Teachers not currently in the classroom or who teach in another area may borrow a class to use for the video required for Component 2. The MOC focus is on how you have grown professionally and positively impacted student learning since your original certification.

WHAT WORKS!

Read the MOC Instructions and all related documents. Understanding what the MOC is designed to elicit and show will create a stronger foundation for the choices you'll make for Components 1 and 2.

Chapter Two

Get Ready!

You've reviewed the Five Core Propositions. You've refreshed your understanding of National Board Standards in your certificate area. You've re-examined the Architecture of Accomplished Teaching and the scoring rubric. What to do next? Now is the time to take some concrete steps to prepare for the process. Here is a suggested sequence of steps to consider:

1. Become familiar with the National Board Website at https://www.nbpts.org/. Look for the Maintenance of Certification tab.
2. Read the MOC Instructions document (https://www.nbpts.org/wp-content/uploads/MOC_Instructions.pdf) multiple times. Pay attention to the glossary of MOC terms within it (Appendix C).
3. Familiarize yourself with the charts, tables, and documents within the instructions.
4. Begin to gather supplies, organize computer files, find evidence that supports your Professional Growth Experiences (PGEs), and present Samples of Products (SOPs) to support both your PGEs and your Written Commentary.

These documents and resources become the go-to places for mapping your way through the MOC process. Becoming familiar with them will save considerable time and grief. Knowing where to go quickly for information is an important way to work smart!

WHAT WORKS! ORGANIZE YOUR TIME

Figuring out how to organize your time is, for many, the biggest challenge of all. You are incredibly busy both at school and at home with work that will continually compete for your time, energy, and attention. Although the MOC process requires less time than either your original certification or the previous renewal process, organizing your time is important. Here are some strategies to manage the demands of the MOC process.

- Just for now, say no! Eliminate as many committee and school responsibilities as possible. Promise your principal you'll be back next year but minimize extracurricular commitments.
- Just for now, cut back at home too. Delegate chores and activities.
- Set aside regular work and writing periods. Some MOC candidates put a spouse/partner in charge on Saturday or Sunday afternoons or one night each week. Others stay late at school one or two days a week or work in their classroom over the weekend. This is extra important from January to the submission date, when work is more labor-intensive and the deadline looms.
- At the very least, don't ADD responsibilities to your schedule at this time.
- Create a flexible timeline and stick to it.

More Strategies

- Avoid procrastination. It will come back to haunt you. You remember from your original experience that during the National

Board process you can't just dash off a paper and produce quality work. MOC requires amassing evidence of your professional growth over time since you certified or last renewed. The MOC process is too complex to be done in a hurry.

- Be aware you'll need to work on more than one aspect of MOC simultaneously.

Why This Works

Organizing your time wisely can be a make-or-break factor in the quality of your submission. Time management figures importantly into keeping a sane work-family balance.

WHAT WORKS! ORGANIZE YOUR MATERIALS AND RESOURCES

You will accumulate mounds of papers and materials during the months you work on MOC.

You'll collect evidence of professional development you have done since you originally certified. You'll collect notes, emails, samples of products, student work samples, and many other pieces of evidence. You'll need a system for collecting and holding these pieces as you decide which to submit. You will want to print your MOC directions for easy reference and so that you can write on them as you think and work. Use the KISS system: **Keep It** Simple, **Silly!** Consider:

- Large notebooks/binders
- Accordion folders
- A folder system
- Box(es) for sorting and depositing papers

Build a Support System

Compared to years past, much more support is available to candidates now. Many schools, districts, and counties that offer cohorts for National Board candidates certifying for the first time also welcome MOC candidates. Investigate such cohorts in your area. Popular accessible resources are National Board Facebook pages, of which there are many. For MOC candidates, the most useful may be the pages called Renewing NBCTs and MOC and NBPTS Renewal Group. It's possible that by the time you read this, the names of these groups could have changed (possibly removing *Renewal*) so use the search box to find MOC groups if these names don't work.

Why These Work

Getting organized with a system that is user-friendly will make you feel more secure moving forward. Collaborating with others gives you a sounding board and a place to ask questions and hear others' perspectives.

WHAT WORKS! PLAN A TIMELINE

Planning a timeline can add stability and consistency to your MOC work. Having a timeline can be a motivator to make a schedule and stick to it. To make a usable timeline, chunk out the pieces of the MOC. Make your timeline flexible but with some boundaries. Begin with Component 1, parse it out, then do the same with Component 2. The components are discussed in upcoming chapters, but here is a flexible, sample timeline to consider:

Fall:

• Brainstorm and list possible Professional Growth Experiences (PGEs).

- Use the Component 1 prompts to help you choose PGEs that will have evidence you can use to respond to the prompts. Use the checklist on page 5 of the MOC Instructions document.
- Apply the sticky note strategy described in chapter 4.
- Collect evidence and Samples of Products for Component 1.
- Begin the Written Commentary for Component 1. Look for someone to read your commentary and give feedback.
- Edit and revise Component 1 Written Commentary drafts several times.

Late Fall/Winter:

- Begin planning Component 2.
- Make plans to borrow a class in your original certificate area if needed. Go into the class to observe a few times to get to know the students. Be sure students are within the age range of your original certificate area.
- Plan to teach and film lessons related to your original certificate area.
- Film multiple lessons to give yourself a choice of which to submit.
- Use the prompts you'll respond to in order to guide your planning.
- Begin the Written Commentary for Component 2.

Late Winter/Spring:

- Continue editing/revising drafts of Component 1 and Component 2 Written Commentaries.
- View the videos you made and choose the segment(s) you want to submit.
- Ask readers to give feedback.
- Edit/revise your writing and complete all forms.

Why This Works

Constructing a flexible timeline will keep you on track and help you avoid procrastination. Procrastination is your enemy.

Chapter Three

Overview, Review, and Evaluation

OVERVIEW

National Board Certified Teachers who completed the process before 2017 had certificates that were active for ten years. They could complete the National Board (NB) renewal process which renewed their certificates for ten years from their current certificate's expiration date. The renewal process consisted of three components that described, analyzed, and reflected on four Professional Growth Experiences. The teachers demonstrated the application of those PGEs through writing, videos, samples of student work, and reflection.

In recent years, many states have changed their licensure requirements, so the National Board developed a new process called Maintenance of Certification (MOC) to more fully align with these systems. Beginning with the 2020–2021 cycle, NBCTs who certified in 2017 or later will complete this new MOC pathway rather than the old renewal process. Successfully completing the MOC extends an NBCT's certification by five years, which aligns with licensure requirements for most states. For example, an NBCT whose certification expires in 2022 is eligible to do the MOC process in 2021, but the new expiration date will be 2027 (five years from 2022, *not* five years from 2021). Through MOC, Board Certified Teachers show they have maintained their professional growth and strong impact on student learning.

The MOC process is much more cost-effective than the previous renewal process at $495 (at the time of publication) plus a $75 registration fee. MOC is consistent with the National Board's mission to make Board Certification as affordable, flexible, and accessible as possible. Like the original certifying process to become an NBCT, MOC has been developed by teachers for teachers. MOC was vetted by NBCTs who undertook a pilot version before the final version was released.

The foundation of MOC, like the original certification process, is based on the Five Core Propositions, the National Board Standards in your certificate area, and the Architecture of Accomplished Teaching (AAT). It is these documents against which the MOC is evaluated. Candidates demonstrate that their teaching practice remains consistent with the high standards that National Board Certification represents.

The MOC Process

The Maintenance of Certificate process is shorter and less comprehensive than what you experienced when you were a first-time candidate. There are two interrelated components in the MOC, for which you will:

- *Demonstrate* that your teaching practice continues the rigor of the original process
- *Show* leadership, collaboration, learning, reflective practice, and professionalism
- *Prepare* written components that document your practice
- *Focus* on Professional Growth Experiences
- *Make* one video connected to one PGE that reflects your practice within your original certificate area

Component 1 Requirements

- Identify two PGEs where you describe how you learned something new that has influence within or beyond the classroom and has a direct or indirect impact on student learning.
- Develop a Written Commentary in response to prompts and evidence that supports that commentary and demonstrates a positive impact on student learning. For each PGE you describe, analyze and reflect on how the PGE continues to align with the Five Core Propositions, the current National Board Standards in your certificate area, and the AAT.
- Collect evidence that supports your PGEs and Written Commentary and demonstrates positive impact on student learning.

Component 2 Requirements

- Choose 1 PGE from Component 1 to demonstrate its application with a group of rostered students who are within the developmental level and content area of your original certification.
- Plan a lesson related to this PGE (same content area and age level as your original certification).
- Prepare a video of no more than ten minutes of you teaching the lesson to a group of students. This group should be in a pre-K through 12 setting in your or a colleague's classroom, school library, gym, virtual class, etc.
- Develop a Written Commentary in response to prompts.

Including the "3 Cs" of Evidence in Your Writing

- *Clear*: Anyone who reads your work should be able to understand what you're saying. You'll explain acronyms and educational jargon. The sequence can be easily followed. Your writing is readable and makes sense.
- *Consistent*: Your writing needs an element of continuity. Don't contradict yourself. Make connections.

- *Convincing*: Present the case that you are an accomplished teacher. This means the evidence you present is believable and achievable. Back up claims with specific examples, documentation, and verification. EVIDENCE = EXAMPLES.

NBCTs have two opportunities to extend their certification: 1) the *year before* their current certification expires; or 2) the *same year* their certification expires. MOC reports include feedback statements if an NBCT is *not* successful. If a teacher submits MOC evidence the year *before* current certification expires, and that evidence does not meet the requirements, the statements can be used as guidelines to strengthen a *second* MOC attempt. Certification is extended for five years from the date of current certification. There are no limits to the number of times an NBCT can extend certification by meeting MOC requirements. *Note*: If you are submitting during the period of COVID-19 exceptions, check the National Board website for current COVID updates and accommodations.

REVIEW

It's now been several years since you originally certified to become an NBCT, or since your last MOC submission, or up to ten years since you renewed under the previous process. While working to become certified or maintain/renew your certification, you demonstrated how your teaching practice addressed the Five Core Propositions, the National Board Standards for your certificate area, and AAT. MOC keeps these documents at the forefront of the process. Before you begin, it may be time to review them in detail.

The Five Core Propositions

The Five Core Propositions describe the core characteristics of an accomplished teacher. They define the knowledge, skills, attitudes, and commitments accomplished teachers demonstrate. They are at the center of the evaluation incorporated in the National Board Certification process and hence in MOC.

1. Teachers are committed to students and their learning.
2. Teachers know the subjects they teach and how to teach those subjects to students.
3. Teachers are responsible for managing and monitoring student learning.
4. Teachers think systematically about their practice and learn from experience.
5. Teachers are members of learning communities.

The National Board Standards Are Your Answer Book!

The National Board Standards reflect the Five Core Propositions. They describe in detail the knowledge, skills, and dispositions that support accomplished practice; illustrate ways professional judgment is reflected in action; and describe how these characteristics could be expressed in a variety of settings. *Note*: Some certificate area Standards have been updated, so be sure you use the current version, which is available on the National Board website. Each certificate area has its own set of Standards. While some themes carry across all certificates, each certificate area has Standards tailored to the unique elements of each. Names of the Standards vary across certificate areas.

Together, the Five Core Propositions and the National Board Standards inform your preparation and development of the PGEs you choose for MOC. Together, they:

- Provide a framework/structure for collecting relevant evidence of your teaching practice.
- Offer guidelines to help you focus your analysis and writing about your practice.

- Clarify your understanding of how your PGEs/MOC process will be evaluated.

Architecture of Accomplished Teaching

The AAT is the National Board version of an accomplished lesson and/or unit plan. It is represented by a spiraling double helix to show six tightly woven "stages" or steps that are ultimately connected to the Five Core Propositions. The AAT graphic is shown in the General Portfolio Instructions on the NBPTS website and on page 9 of the MOC Instructions document. The graphic is an underused tool that can greatly add to understanding the prompts you'll respond to in your MOC Instructions. When looking at the AAT graphic, "read" it from the bottom up.

WHAT WORKS! Analyzing the AAT

The stages and matching propositions, from beginning to end, are:

1. *Know your students*: Who are they? Where are they now? What do they need and in what order do they need it? Where should I begin? (Proposition 1)
2. *Set high, worthwhile goals* appropriate for *these students*, at *this time*, in *this setting.* How do the goals you set connect to your National Board Standards and MOC directions? How do the goals fit into your instructional sequence? What do you want your students to know and be able to do at the end of the lesson/unit of study? (Proposition 1)
3. *Implement instruction* designed to attain those goals. What approaches/strategies/techniques/activities do you plan to use that will accomplish the goals? In what sequence might you use these planned strategies? How will these support your students' learning? What is your rationale for implementing instruction this way? What criteria might you use to decide if and when to use another strategy? (Proposition 2)

4. *Evaluate learning* in light of the goals and the instruction. How will you assess student learning? Why did you choose this/these method(s) for these students at this time, in this setting? What evidence will let you know the instruction was successful—or not? What, if anything, did the assessments tell you about your instruction? Where will you go next? (Proposition 3)

5. *Reflect on student learning*, the effectiveness of the instructional design, particular concerns, and issues. How do you know you made the right choices? What was successful and what wasn't? How could students reflect on their own learning? (Proposition 4)

6. *Set new high and worthwhile goals* appropriate for *these students*, at *this time*, in *this setting*. How will you decide when it is time to move on in the lesson/unit sequence? What indicators will you use to set new goals? (Proposition 3)

Note: Proposition 5, though a part of the MOC, is not represented on the AAT.

To simplify, in my *What Works! Successful Strategies for Pursuing National Board Certification* books written for the initial certification process, I present the SSTARS acronym for naming the steps on the AAT. This is applicable to the MOC process, too.

- **S**tudents: Know your students and how they learn. (Proposition 1)
- **S**et high, worthwhile, appropriate goals. (Propositions 1 and 2)
- **T**each using appropriate, effective strategies/activities. (Propositions 2 and 3)
- **A**ssess students' progress using a variety of evaluation types and strategies. (Proposition 3)
- **R**eflect on your teaching and students' progress in order to look ahead. (Proposition 4)
- **S**tart the process over again.

Why This Works

The steps of the AAT provide a complete lesson/unit plan that will have the greatest impact on student learning. Some MOC process prompts reference steps on the AAT, though to a lesser degree than the prompts in your original certification work.

The Evaluation Rubric

The Evaluation Rubric is an important but underutilized resource. The assessors have the rubrics beside them as they evaluate your work. The holistic MOC evaluation process is not a secret! The evidence you need to show is specifically detailed in the rubric.

WHAT WORKS!

Effective tools such as the Five Core Propositions, AAT, SSTARS, and the Evaluation Rubric align to steer you to meaningful responses to the prompts. Make these tools work for you!

EVALUATION

One or more NBCTs will evaluate each MOC submission independently and holistically, evaluating the two components as a single entity. You will not receive a numerical score like you did when you first certified. Based on the entire body of evidence of your submission, an assessor then makes a single decision—to *maintain* or *not to maintain* certification. A trainer reviews and confirms all nonmaintained decisions. Each submission is evaluated according to the criteria listed in the rubric below. Each bullet is considered and applied to your submission. Use these criteria for guidance when choosing materials to submit in order to provide a comprehensive picture of your professional growth since certification.

The MOC Evaluation Rubric

An MOC submission is assessed based on the extent to which it provides *sufficient evidence* of continued professional growth using the following criteria. The candidate must:

- *Identify/address* significant needs of students, communities supporting students, and/or the candidate
- *Acquire and/or deepen* certificate-specific content knowledge and/or pedagogical practice and/or knowledge
- *Effectively integrate* appropriate technology to directly and/or indirectly impact student learning
- *Involve* others in Professional Growth Experiences
- *Practice* National Board Standards–based, relevant, and meaningful instruction in the candidate's certificate area
- *Ensure* fairness, equity of access, and promote appreciation of diversity in the candidate's instructional practice
- *Provide* a meaningful, positive impact on student learning
- *Include* ongoing and varied professional experiences
- *Use* reflection to analyze the connections and patterns in your continuing professional growth

Evaluation Summary

Together, the two components present sufficient evidence of professional growth and positive impact on student learning since certification, previous renewal, or the last successful completion of MOC. Although there may be unevenness in the level of evidence presented, overall there is sufficient evidence of professional growth and positive impact on student learning that continues to align with the Five Core Propositions, the current National Board Standards for the candidate's area of certification, and the Architecture of Accomplished Teaching.

- All components are evaluated as one entity.

- Assessors review all the evidence you submit for both components against the criteria in the rubric.
- You will receive a single *decision*—rather than a numerical score—informing whether you maintained or did not maintain certification.
- If you receive a decision that you maintained certification, no feedback is given.
- If you receive a decision that you did not maintain certification, your submission will be reviewed by a scoring leader to ensure fairness and accuracy. Scoring leaders have the authority to overturn a decision of not maintaining certification if deemed necessary and appropriate.
- If you receive a decision that you did not maintain certification, you will receive feedback indicating one or more aspects of your submission that needed strengthening (e.g., "In identification of relevant needs, you need to strengthen the level of evidence you provided").

Reliability, Accuracy, and Fairness

Yearly, the National Board conducts analyses to determine the level of assessor reliability (i.e., level of agreement between independent assessors). The results of these analyses have consistently indicated that National Board assessors make reliable, accurate, and fair evaluations of candidates' responses. The NBPTS consistently evaluates its assessments and the assessment process with the goal of continuous improvement. The National Board is committed to making sure its assessments have validity, are meaningful, and that the evaluation of candidates' responses is reliable, accurate, and fair.

The NS Designation

If the decision on your Score Report indicates "NS" (not scorable), then one or more of the following may apply:

- You did not submit one, or both, of the two MOC Components.
- You registered in the online system but didn't submit any artifacts to be scored, OR there is missing evidence such as the video recording, the Written Commentaries, or the Samples of Product, OR you uploaded the wrong materials for either component.
- Your Component 2 submission revealed the age range requirement was not met, OR the class/groups featured did not include at least 51 percent of students within the defined ages of your certificate area.
- Your Component 2 submission featured content that did not fall within the scope of your certificate area.
- You were not seen and heard interacting with students in at least one segment of the Component 2 video.
- Your students were not seen and heard in the Component 2 video.
- You were suspected of plagiarism or cheating.

WHAT WORKS!

Plan backwards! Read and study the Evaluation Rubric before planning your components during the period you are working on the Written Commentary and the video, as you reflect and revise, and again before you submit. Planning backwards assures that you're aware of all the requirements and what must be present in order for the assessor(s) to evaluate your work.

Chapter Four

Component 1

Developing Your Professional Growth Experiences

RATIONALE

Teaching reaches beyond the walls of individual classrooms into the wider communities of learning. As accomplished teachers, NBCTs address learning, professional, and community needs and continue to refine their own teaching skills and practice. To do this, NBCTs become involved in a broad range of content, pedagogical, and professional knowledge and expertise. They often participate in a collegial approach that contributes significantly to the quality of their practice, the school environment, and student learning. NBCTs are often on the front lines of new learning and trends, leading the way rather than resisting learning that requires change.

MOC COMPONENT 1 IN A NUTSHELL

- *Identify* two Professional Growth Experiences (PGEs) that relate to your *original certificate area* in which you are engaged and that resulted in either direct or indirect positive impacts on student learning.

- One PGE must be used for/applied to the certification-specific video lesson in Component 2, discussed in chapter 6.
- *Develop* a Written Commentary in response to specific prompts.
- *Collect* evidence (Samples of Products) that supports your PGEs and Written Commentary.
- *Collect* evidence that demonstrates impact on student learning.

WHAT IS A PROFESSIONAL GROWTH EXPERIENCE?

A Professional Growth Experience is an activity in which you learned something new that has influence within or beyond the classroom and has had a direct or indirect impact on student learning. A PGE will reflect a continuous commitment and contributions to professional activities that ultimately impact student learning.

A PGE will showcase activities that have been the focus of a teacher's growth over an extended period of time. It will reflect an NBCT's resourcefulness and initiative in taking advantage of opportunities to achieve goals, improve practices, and affect the wider school community. PGEs showcase NBCTs as lifelong learners. These experiences may have begun before your certification or at a later point but have evolved to become an important focus of your professional growth during this current MOC cycle (since initial certification or renewal or since completing MOC, whichever is most recent and relevant to your situation). PGEs address a need held by stakeholders: the teacher, the students, the community, or the district.

Per the Evaluation Rubric, together, the two PGEs must demonstrate that you:

- *Identify and address* relevant needs of students, communities supporting students (e.g., the professional community, families), and/or yourself
- *Acquire and/or deepen* certificate-specific knowledge and/or pedagogical practice and/or knowledge

- *Effectively integrate* appropriate technology to directly and/or indirectly impact student learning
- *Involve* others in PGEs
- *Practice* National Board Standards–based, relevant, and meaningful instruction
- *Ensure* fairness and equity of access and promote appreciation of diversity in your practice
- *Provide* meaningful, positive, direct and/or indirect impacts on student learning
- *Provide* ongoing and varied professional experiences
- *Use* reflection to analyze the connections and patterns in your continuing professional growth

Examples of PGEs

PGEs can "look" many different ways. Many candidates begin with broad categories. *Broad* category examples include:

- Social-emotional learning
- Equity
- Leadership
- STEM (science, technology, engineering, math)
- Technology
- Family engagement
- Curriculum
- Literacy
- Collaboration
- Assessment
- Endorsements
- Content learning
- Community
- Mental health/trauma
- Teaching strategies
- Teacher quality

One strategy is to start with specific activities you've done that have had a direct and/or indirect positive impact on student learning. PGEs that are more *specific* might include:

- Book studies
- Textbook/curriculum trainings
- Analysis of data training
- Parent nights/academies
- Online/in-person cohort
- Newsletter
- Grant writing
- Weekend book bags
- Before- and after-school tutoring
- Content-related workshops
- Cognitive coaching
- Professional learning community (PLC)
- Behavior workshops
- Mentoring/coaching new teachers
- Your role in significant projects
- Needs analysis
- Research projects
- Collaboration with colleagues
- Website creation
- Family/community events

CHOOSING YOUR PGES

Brainstorm a list of possible PGEs. Note the year(s) each occurred. Gather attendance certificates, notes you took while attending, agendas, lesson plans you used to implement your learning, and other materials. Choose experiences that helped reshape your thinking and teaching, such as:

- School, district, state leadership roles, including committees

- Workshops and trainings
- Conferences you've attended and/or presented at, including professional development that *you* presented to staff
- Collaboration activities
- New strategies you learned and applied
- New technology you learned and applied
- Ways you communicate with families

Analyze your list to see if you can find any patterns. It's likely several of your PGEs will fit together to form some categories. Some might fit into more than one category. For example:

- If you participated in several Google trainings, those could fit under technology.
- If you underwent a phonics training, a Lucy Calkins training, or an online class on "Choosing Literature Studies," those could fit with curriculum, literacy, content-related workshops, and/or content learning.
- If you've been trained to become a mentor or coach, these might address leadership and/or teacher quality.

The Sticky Note Strategy

There are two options for organizing a strategy using sticky notes: 1) begin with activities, group them together, then assign a category name to the group; or 2) begin with category names, then match individual activities with the category.

Directions for Option 1:

- After brainstorming a list of possible PGEs, write each PGE activity you've completed/attended since certification (or your previous renewal) on a separate sticky note. Consider classes, workshops, book studies, research, learning through committee work, and other activities. It's helpful to add the year the activity occurred. *You may go back before your initial certification, re-*

newal, or previous MOC period. Check the instructions for details.

- Stack the sticky notes that relate to each other in piles or columns. The goal is to form several piles/columns, each of which could become a PGE. Though you'll only write about two PGEs, it's a good idea to brainstorm several so that you can choose the strongest. A PGE can also be a single experience as long as it meets the MOC criteria. Some sticky notes might not fit into any category; it's ok not to use them all.
- Look at the piles/columns. Can you find a category name that would fit those activities? The category name would be broader than the more specific activities.
- That learning became a focus because of a need: *your* need, a *district* need, a *student* need. Identify the need you were meeting when you did that learning.
- Now you're ready to choose and write your PGEs. You'll be able to identify the need, what you did to address the need, and describe the impact on student learning.

Directions for Option 2: Just reverse the order. Begin with the category names, then match each activity to the category. Either way, you end up with a list of PGE categories and activities.

WHAT WORKS! More about Choosing Your PGEs

- *Avoid* choosing experiences that were "one and done." If you went to a workshop and it was great but didn't lead to other impactful experiences, then it may not be a strong choice.
- *Choose* PGEs that had an ongoing impact. For example, a candidate went to a summer institute to learn how to address poor writing skills. What he learned shifted his pedagogy about writing and grammar. He shared his learning with his professional learning community, then planned a professional development workshop for his staff. This led to completing an action research

project, which he presented the following year at a conference. This PGE represented experiences that were ongoing, multifaceted, and didn't just end when the summer institute ended.

WHAT WORKS! Begin with the End in Mind: Start with the Prompts

If you know where you're going, you're more likely to choose an effective route. *Where you're going*, in this case, is to address the Component 1 prompts and give clear, consistent, convincing evidence for each. Let's look at those prompts, which are divided into Set 1 and Set 2. As you read each prompt, note how the language of the Evaluation Rubric is often embedded.

Set 1: Respond for *each* PGE:

1. Provide a context of the professional situation that indicates what relevant need(s) of students, the professional community, parents/guardians, and/or yourself you are addressing with your PGE.
2. Identify your PGE (e.g., provide a title), describe your PGE, and explain how your PGE demonstrates a response to the identified need(s).
3. In the context of your PGE, explain how you acquired and deepened your certificate area-specific content knowledge and/or your pedagogical knowledge and skills to remain current, including use of research and/or use of other professional activities.
4. Analyze ways in which your PGE and related activities positively impacted student learning whether directly or indirectly.
5. Reflect on the PGE presented, including the steps, milestones, or goals you accomplished through this PGE, and changes, additions, and/or next steps that would enhance your professional growth in the future.

Set 2: Respond to the following prompts for *one* or *both* of your PGEs:

1. Describe how you have effectively integrated technology into your practice.
2. Explain how you have ensured fairness and equity of access and promoted appreciation of diversity among the students and the learning community.
3. Explain how your interaction with colleagues, other professional groups, parents, and/or community members has enhanced your professional growth.
4. In the broader context of your PGEs and your practice, analyze patterns or themes that have emerged that define you as an educator as you reflect on your professional growth since certification.

Set 2 prompts must be applied *somewhere* within the Component 1 Written Commentary. They could apply to both PGEs, or just one, as long as they all have a response.

Now the task is to look at the PGEs/activities you have grouped together and ascertain whether they're usable, meaning whether they provide evidence (examples) for the responses, using the following steps:

1. Make sure each PGE you consider provides evidence for comprehensive responses to the Set 1 prompts. If not, discard any PGE that doesn't meet that criteria and choose another.
2. Decide which PGEs could apply to one or more of the Set 2 prompts. For each Set 2 prompt, list the PGEs that could supply evidence for it. As long as each prompt has at least one PGE connected to it, it is a usable PGE. You can do this by creating a checklist or a simple two-column chart. There are checklists for Component 1 and Component 2 on pages 26 and 27 of the MOC Instructions document. If any Set 2

prompt is left without evidence, then you'll need to consider other PGEs. Eventually, you'll find two PGEs that give evidence for all the prompts. Be sure you can connect all PGEs to their impact on student learning. Those PGEs are keepers!

Table 4.1 gives examples of PGEs representing various teaching levels rather than those of a single teacher. As a sorting exercise, look at each category and accompanying activities and think about which two might have all the elements needed to respond comprehensively to both Set 1 and Set 2 prompts. That is your goal—to come up with two PGEs that can provide evidence for *all* the prompts.

SAMPLE PGE SCENARIOS

Scenario #1: Parent Engagement

Rick is a middle school Language Arts teacher with 15 years of experience. He also teaches a cluster of English-language learners (ELL). Rick recently moved to a different school. He didn't know the school demographic well and particularly felt that he needed to do a better job engaging parents. Since his initial National Board Certification, Rick:

- Held several discussions with his principal
- Developed an interactive newsletter for parents, sharing information about the classroom and asking for input from parents/caregivers
- Established a quarterly evening activity for parents based on a current topic of study
- Invited parents into the classroom during the instructional day
- Enrolled in Spanish lessons because most of his ELL students were native Spanish speakers so he could communicate better with parents

Table 4.1. Sample PGE Sorting Exercise: High School/Middle School/Elementary

PGE Category	Example Activities
Curriculum	AVID course training, 2015–2016
	AVID Site Team Committee, 2016–2018
	Implementation of AVID classes, 2016–present
	IB course training, 2014–present
	Teach IB curriculum, 2015–present
Family Engagement	Home visits, 2016–present
	Drop-in office hours, 2018–present
	Quarterly Parent Academies, 2018–present
	Weekend book bag buddies, 2015–present
STEM	Online cohort, 2019–present
	District cohort, 2017–2018
	90 hours of professional development through Discovery Ed, 2017–2019
	Professional learning community collaboration to create STEM-integrated, project-based learning activities, 2017–present
	Monthly STEM newsletter, 2017– present
Technology	Professional development training: "SAFE" lessons, 2018
	Professional development training: Digital Citizen Responsibilities, 2018
	Professional development training: Google Classroom, 2019
	Professional development training: Literacy websites including BrainPOP, BookBub, and Reading Rockets, 2019
Literacy	New textbook training, 2017
	Collaboration with Literacy team, 2017–present
	Read to Succeed training, 2018
	College Career Standards Conference, 2016
	Advanced Placement training, 2019

Scenario #2: Technology

Rosa, a high school math teacher with eight years of experience, has worked to improve her computer skills so that she can be a resource to her students when they use computers for their course work. Since she originally certified, Rosa:

- Participated in a five-day workshop highlighting several math websites
- Took a higher level course at a community college
- Collaborated with her department professional learning community to develop lessons based on computer use
- Integrated computer use into her unit instruction
- Used her learning to give a presentation at a faculty meeting

Scenario #3: Literacy

Roxanne is a first grade teacher who wanted to become more expert in teaching her literacy curriculum. She had taught in the primary grades for 15 years. She was beginning to feel "stale" and wanted to improve and refresh her teaching knowledge and pedagogy. Here are some actions Roxanne took since her initial National Board Certification:

- Attended a state literacy conference for the past three years
- Used materials from the conferences in her literacy lessons
- Enrolled in a master's program in literacy and earned her degree
- Moved into a literacy coaching position within her district
- Worked with committees to update the primary grades literacy curriculum in her district

WHAT WORKS! Analyze YOUR Story

Think back over the time period between either your original certification or your previous renewal or MOC decision (whichever was the more recent) and brainstorm literally every activity, every training, every collaboration opportunity in which you participated. Go through your file cabinet and folders to find certificates of attendance, lesson plan books, calendars, and other artifacts that indicate these activities and opportunities. Make lists of activities, their dates, and "nutshell" descriptions.

- Think of WHAT the activities were.
- Think of WHY you participated in these activities.
- Think about WHAT NEED this activity addressed.
- Think of WHAT you learned.
- Think about HOW you implemented the learning with your students.
- Think about HOW collaboration might have played a role.
- Think about HOW each impacted student learning.

Collecting Evidence to Support Your PGEs

You will write about each PGE and its accompanying activities in a Written Commentary. However, for each PGE, you will also collect and submit Samples of Products (SOPs). Although the PGE may have occurred earlier, the SOP must be collected *in the year you apply for MOC*. Select the strongest SOPs that provide evidence, clarification, and/or enhancement of the activities within the PGE. SOPs may include, but are not limited to, the following:

- Student work samples
- Letters/attestations from colleagues, parents, students, community members
- Representative pages from a course evaluation
- Notes from learning experiences

Why These Work

Doing these sorting exercises for yourself, with your own brainstormed list, should yield strong PGEs that provide evidence of your ongoing commitment or contribution to the profession and demonstrate continued application of the NBPTS in your practice. PGEs should be multifaceted and connect to your certification-specific knowledge, professional development, current trends in the field, and interactions with colleagues, other professionals, and families.

Chapter Five

Component 1

Written Commentary and Samples of Products

OVERVIEW

For Component 1, you will:

- *Develop* a Written Commentary based on two sets of prompts.
- *Describe, analyze, and reflect* on how your two PGEs and your practice continue to align with the Five Core Propositions, the *current* National Board Standards for your certificate area, and the Architecture of Accomplished Teaching.
- *Provide* evidence that the two PGEs *together* address the Component 1 prompts.
- *Show* how you positively impacted student learning through your professional growth.
- *Provide* evidence through Samples of Products (SOPs) you've gathered since your original certification or most recent MOC or renewal.
- *Explain* how each SOP connects to one or both PGEs. To be considered and assessed with your Written Commentary, the SOPs must be collected during the *current* MOC period.

• *Refer* to each SOP and explain their relevance in the Written Commentary.

THE WRITTEN COMMENTARY (WC)

Unlike when you originally certified or renewed, you do not create your own word-processing document for the MOC process. The National Board has created a Written Commentary template, available for download on the website's MOC page, that meets all the formatting requirements such as font, line spacing, and margins (11-point Arial, double-spaced, 1-inch margins)—one less set of worries! *Do not modify the settings.* You must stay within the eight-page maximum. A WC with more than eight pages won't be read or evaluated. If you create the WC in another way, in another program, then copy it into the template, being sure it still meets all formatting requirements. *Save the template* in a secure place where you can retrieve it easily to continue work or submit it. Spell out terms the first time you use them. Use acronyms sparingly. Excessive use of acronyms can hinder assessors' understanding and could have a negative impact on your MOC decision. Note there is also a Component 1 Cover Sheet.

Probing the Component 1 Prompts

The prompts are designed to: 1) guide you to provide relevant information about your PGEs; 2) elicit information about your practice that connects to the AAT, the National Board Standards, and the Five Core Propositions; and 3) give you the opportunity to provide evidence of component requirements. Note that language from the Evaluation Rubric is embedded within many prompts. There are two sets of prompts.

Set 1: Respond for *each* PGE:

1. Provide a context of the professional situation that indicates what relevant need(s) of students, the professional community, parents/guardians, and/or yourself you are addressing with your PGE.
2. Identify your PGE (e.g., provide a title), describe your PGE, and explain how your PGE demonstrates a response to the identified need(s).
3. In the context of your PGE, explain how you acquired and deepened your certificate area–specific content knowledge and/or your pedagogical knowledge and skills to remain current, including use of research and/or use of other professional activities.
4. Analyze ways in which your PGE and related activities positively impacted student learning whether directly or indirectly.
5. Reflect on the PGE presented, including the steps, milestones, or goals you accomplished through this PGE, and changes, additions, and/or next steps that would enhance your professional growth in the future.

Set 2: Respond to the following prompts for *one* or *both* of your PGEs:

1. Describe how you have effectively integrated technology into your practice.
2. Explain how you have ensured fairness and equity of access and promoted appreciation of diversity among the students and the learning community.
3. Explain how your interaction with colleagues, other professional groups, parents, and/or community members has enhanced your professional growth.
4. In the broader context of your PGEs and your practice, analyze patterns or themes that have emerged that define you as

an educator as you reflect on your professional growth since certification.

WHAT WORKS!

- Clearly identify each PGE. Give each a short title you refer to in the WC, such as "Grant Writing," "Mentoring First-Year Teachers," or "Piloting Technology for the Science Classroom."
- Respond to all the prompts for the first PGE, then all the prompts about the second PGE. Don't bounce back and forth between the two (i.e., respond to prompts 1–5 about your first PGE and then respond to prompts 1–5 for your second PGE) as this could impede the assessors' understanding of the WC and have a negative effect on the MOC decision.
- Prompts 1–5 must be addressed for *each/both* of the PGEs.
- Prompts 6–9 must be addressed *somewhere* in the WC for *one or both* PGEs.
- Do not include the prompts within the text of your WC.
- Further formatting specifications are detailed in the National Board MOC Instructions document. Become familiar with them!

WHAT WORKS! Reflection

Because reflection is integral to your mission as an NBCT, reflection is an important element within the MOC process. Your reflection will be part of the Written Commentaries you compose for Component 1 and Component 2. Component 1 reflection focuses on the two PGEs you selected. Component 2 reflection relates more specifically to the lesson and video you prepare.

Do not skimp on the reflection prompts. Reflection is a special type of analysis that looks back in order to look forward. Reflection prompts are highly evidential. Respond comprehensively!

SAMPLES OF PRODUCTS

Samples of Products are the evidence you present in support of each PGE. They must be strongly connected to the PGEs and the Written Commentary's analysis and reflection. This evidence is gathered during this current MOC cycle (since your certification or renewal, or since your last MOC, whichever is most recent and applies to your situation). Consider carefully what samples will, together with your Written Commentary, best document your PGEs. SOPs should illustrate the direct and/or indirect positive impact you made on student learning. Direct evidence might include student work, while indirect evidence might come from collaborations with colleagues, families, and/or the broader community.

Examples of SOPs (not limited to):

- Student work samples/products (e.g., writing, artwork, self-reflections on learning)
- Photos of three-dimensional work products and nontext work (e.g., artwork, engineering projects) or students engaged in learning activities
- Test data or other measures of student performance
- Testimonials from teachers/other staff regarding impact on student learning related to implementation of the training/mentoring you provided
- Emails from families/colleagues/staff members
- Quantitative or qualitative data connected to student engagement or attitudes toward learning
- Attendance/graduation rates
- Results/outcomes for particular student populations/subgroups
- Data related to the use of resources (e.g., library, technology) in support of student learning
- Excerpts from a blog, website, article, or paper that you wrote/created

- Summary of the results of a project you worked on or implemented

You must explain *how* the SOP is connected to the PGE(s) and *how* it demonstrates impact on student learning. Consider that, although a certificate or transcript shows your participation in professional development or coursework, it may not show your impact on student learning.

SOP Tips

- *Create* a separate file for the SOPs.
- *Submit* no more than two pages of evidence per PGE.
- Sequentially, *add* short names/titles to each SOP in the file.
- *Use* numbers or names to clarify your references to particular SOPs in the Written Commentary.
- *Provide* only evidence you collected during your current MOC period.

COMPONENT 1 RESOURCES

Within the MOC Instructions document are several resources that will help you make choices and ensure that you meet the requirements for Component 1. They contain many important details. Spend time studying them so your component will be complete.

Page 17: Allowable Period for Component 1 Evidence Collection

Pages 18–20: Component 1 Specifications for Written Materials and Evidence

Pages 26–27: Component 1 Checklist

Page 29: Electronic Submission at a Glance

Pages 30–32: Appendix A: Writing about Your Practice

Pages 35–38: Appendix C: Maintenance of Certification–Related Terms

Chapter Six

Component 2

The Video Component

RATIONALE

Teachers in and out of the classroom, as well as counselors, mentors, and coaches, are lifelong learners of their craft, seeking to expand their toolbox of strategies, deepen their content knowledge and skills, and hone their instructional decisions to have further impact on student learning. "Students" can refer to those who are of school age or adult learners. NBCTs regularly respond to their students' diversity in a fair and equitable manner, using their knowledge of students to create a positive learning environment. Teachers have a professional obligation to be inventive in their teaching, recognize the need to seek out current findings and trends, and stand ready to incorporate appropriate ideas and methods that fit their goals and benefit their students.

MOC COMPONENT 2 IN A NUTSHELL

- *Choose one* PGE featured in Component 1 and demonstrate its application with a rostered group of students. During the COVID-19 period, the National Board modified the meaning of *ros-*

tered, so during your candidacy, check the NBPTS website to verify the current definition.

- *Prepare* a 10-minute video lesson that is date-stamped or validated with an Attestation Form in which you demonstrate teaching content from the *same* certificate area and developmental age range as your original certificate. This video can be divided into three segments and filmed on multiple days. You choose the length of each segment for a minimum of 10 minutes.
- *Show* student learning, in both the video and the Written Commentary, in an environment that ensures equity of access, promotes an appreciation of diversity, and demonstrates certificate-specific content.
- *Respond* to the specific prompts listed for Component 2.
- *Appear* and *be heard and identifiable* in at least one segment of the video. The segments should show the teacher and the students and students interacting with the teacher and each other.

More about Component 2

- The purpose of the lesson must showcase the application of *one* PGE from Component 1.
- Fifty-one percent of the class must meet the age/developmental requirements of your *original* certificate at the time the video is made.
- The context for the lesson might include socioeconomic factors that impact student learning, technology availability, student age and developmental levels, and/or special-needs groups such as English-language learners.
- The class you are teaching for the video may be that of a colleague. During the COVID-19 period, some blending of classes is/was allowed. *Check the COVID-19 page* on the NBPTS website to see the current allowances.
- Instructional materials are not required for Component 2 and will not be evaluated if submitted.

- The video may not exceed 10 minutes. It may be *continuous* (unedited) or it may be *segmented* into a maximum of three parts, but *within* each segment, there can be no editing.
- The students must be rostered, although you don't need to be the teacher of record. You may borrow a class.

CONSIDERATIONS FOR PLANNING COMPONENT 2

If you are teaching in the classroom, in the same content area as your original certificate, you are good to go! Your students will fit the age requirements of your original certificate.

If you are no longer in the classroom:

- If you are an NBCT who is no longer in the classroom, you'll want to establish a relationship with a colleague whose students fit the age range and content area of your original certification. You'll design and deliver instruction that meets the needs of these students and is effectively incorporated into the goals of the instructional plan (which, in turn, is connected to the PGE selected from Component 1). Consider partnering with a newer teacher, then analyze and debrief the video together so that teacher benefits from your experience and expertise.
- The expectation for accomplished teaching practice, as defined in the Five Core Propositions and the Architecture of Accomplished Teaching, is that accomplished teachers must first know the students they are teaching and know the needs of those students before effective instruction can take place.

If you no longer teach in the same certificate area and/or age/ developmental level as your original certification or renewal:

- You must feature a class of students at the same age or developmental level as your *original* area of certification.

- You may need to consider the same recommendations suggested in the scenario above concerning establishing a relationship with a class of students who may not be students whom you are currently teaching.
- Consider team teaching or partnering on a special project that meets the needs of the student population, while also allowing you to showcase an area of your professional growth featured in one of your PGEs from Component 1.

If you are now teaching students at the same age/developmental level but a different content area than your original certification or renewal:

- You must feature a lesson teaching content from your *original* area of certification.
- You may need to consider the recommendations outlined in the scenarios above regarding establishing a rapport with a colleague's class, or you may integrate content from your original certificate area in a meaningful and relevant way into a lesson you are currently teaching.
- Your students must be at the same age and developmental level as your certificate area.

SAMPLE COMPONENT 2 SCENARIOS

Scenario #1: Teaching in the Same Certificate Area

You are good to go! Lynette certified as an Early Childhood Generalist. She still teaches within this certificate area for the same age/developmental level, although she has changed grade levels since certification. The PGE she selected from her MOC Component 1 to use in Component 2 focused on math workshops/trainings/book studies she undertook to improve her math teaching skills. She filmed a math lesson in fractions for Component 2. She also could have used reading, writing, science, or social studies, as these were all parts of her original certificate subject area, *as long as it connected to a PGE from Component 1.*

Scenario #2: No Longer in the Classroom

Amanda holds the early and middle childhood (EMC) Literacy/ Reading/Language Arts certificate and was in a self-contained classroom when she certified. Since certification, she has become a Reading/Literacy Coach and works with the reading and language arts teachers in her building. She both "pushes in" to classrooms and "pulls out" students as needed. She "borrowed" two classes, a primary class and an intermediate class, and taught lessons to both. In the primary class, she worked with sight words. With the intermediate class she focused on visual literacy. In the end she chose the visual literacy video to submit. She divided the video into three segments showing the beginning, middle, and end of the lesson.

Scenario #3: No Longer in the Classroom

Ron certified in adolescent to young adult (AYA) Science. After certifying, he left the classroom to become an assistant principal. For his MOC, he borrowed a sophomore biology class and taught a unit on biomes. He partnered with the teacher for a few class sessions in order to get to know the students, then taught the unit of study. The lesson he submitted was the third lesson within the unit, a lab.

Scenario #4: No Longer at the Same Age/Developmental Level

Sam's certificate area is early adolescence (EA) language arts. When he certified and renewed, he taught seventh and eighth grade Language Arts. Since then, he has moved to a high school (AYA English/Language Arts) where he now teaches Advanced Placement English to seniors. For the MOC video, he collaborated with the ninth grade English teacher on a project she had undertaken. Sam had to plan to complete his teaching with the ninth graders during first semester so that 51 percent of the students would be in the age range of the EA certificate.

Scenario #5: Teaching in a Different Content Area

Jennifer taught eighth grade math in a K–8 school and certified in EA Math. Last year her principal moved her to a seventh grade science position. She filmed her science class for her MOC video, and focused on using math measuring skills in a science lab experiment.

Scenario #6: Teaching in a Different Content Area

Luke taught in a self-contained third grade class and certified as a Middle Childhood Generalist. Right after he renewed, he changed to a sixth grade social studies departmentalized position. He "borrowed" a fourth grade class from a former teammate and taught map-reading skills for his MOC Component 2 video.

THE VIDEO RECORDING

The video for MOC Component 2 need not be as comprehensive as the videos you made for your initial certification. You have already proven yourself to be an accomplished teacher. With this video, you show you have maintained that accomplished status. You are showing that your teaching still aligns with the Five Core Propositions, the *current* National Board Standards for your certificate area, and the Architecture of Accomplished Teaching.

Making the Video

- Submit *one 10-minute* (maximum), date-stamped video recording. Remember, an administrator can attest to the date on the Attestation Form if your camera doesn't have a date stamp.
- The *only allowable edit* is combining up to three segments into one video file before submitting. Within each segment, there can be no other edits. The segments may be recorded on different days if the lesson takes place over multiple days. Segments may be of varying lengths.
- A segment is defined as a *continuous and unedited section* of a video taken from a longer video recording.
- If the video is divided into segments, you must be seen and heard in at least *one* segment. Otherwise your submission won't be evaluated and you'll receive an "NS" (not scorable) designation.
- You and your students must be seen and heard in the video. Assessors need to see you and your students together, students interacting with each other and with you, students' responses to what you're doing, and their engagement in learning. If interactions are minimal or missing, there will be limited evidence to evaluate.

More about Editing

Editing is defined as postproduction processing of the video itself. Examples of editing include breaks in recurring footage or the addition of footage within a segment; adding graphics, titles, or special effects; using fade-ins or fade-outs; muting the audio; adding audio recorded material from a device or audio track other than the video recorder itself; and/or blurring or blocking an image to conceal a face or name tag.

Videos of virtual classrooms can be a split-screen recording, a platform-provided recording such as Google Meet or Microsoft Teams, or a video made with a camera/phone/tablet that captures the teacher at the computer with students on the screen. Because it's important to show interaction between you and the students as well as among the students, icons of students are not sufficient, nor are asynchronous lessons. Lessons must be recorded in real time.

Amplifying sound to enhance the audio of a video recording is acceptable as long as the amplification doesn't conflict with the postproduction editing rules described above and in the MOC directions on the National Board website.

WHAT WORKS! Recording Tips

- *Use* a single camera. Using two cameras to create a "studio" effect is not allowed.
- *Use* a camera angle that includes as many student faces as possible. If filming a group, consider placing the camera near a front "corner," looking diagonally across the class. It's ok to pick up the camera and move it during filming. See the General Portfolio Instructions for filming diagrams and Appendix B in the MOC Instructions for more detailed information.
- *Place* the camera on a tripod if possible.
- It's acceptable to *zoom in* on a particular student or group if they are performing in some way, demonstrating a skill, and/or speaking.
- *Ask* someone to come to your classroom to film for you if possible. Sometimes students can also perform videography well.
- Where possible, *point* the camera at the speaker, whether that be a student or you, the teacher.
- If filming a whiteboard or projected materials, *zoom in* so the writing is visible without glare to the assessor.
- *Make* your room as bright as possible by turning on all lights and opening curtains. However, avoid filming directly into bright light, such as directly toward windows. Try to keep a direct source of light behind the camera.

- If recording a virtual lesson, be sure to *angle* the camera to avoid screen glare.
- *Eliminate* noises that might interfere with recording. Turn off fans, fish-tank filters, and any other noise-causing conditions.
- *Post* a "Do Not Disturb" sign on your door to cut down on interruptions. Also notify the office that you'll be recording. Avoid recording when there might be lawn mowers, recess noise, band practice, or other noise distractions.
- *Place* the microphone as close to the speakers as possible. Consider using an external microphone or wearing a microphone so that if you move close to a student, the microphone goes with you and will pick up the response/conversation. Carry a camera/phone/mic to a location where you want to capture conversation.

Why These Work

While professional quality isn't expected, following the above technical tips will improve the quality of your videos. There are environmental and technical challenges when trying to get good video and sound quality. Making these as clear as possible will help the assessor to interpret the content of the lesson and the dialogue, giving stronger evidence to evaluate.

THE WRITTEN COMMENTARY

To save work, the National Board has created a *template* on which to complete the Component 2 Written Commentary in order to ensure formatting requirements such as font (Arial 11-point), line spacing (double-spaced), and margins (1 inch) are met. The template is available for download on the NBPTS website's MOC page. *Do not modify the settings* of the template in any way, and stay within the page limits (five pages). If you compose your Written Commentary in another file and copy it into the template, be sure it still meets all the formatting requirements. *Save the template* in a secure place (especially if working over multiple sessions) where you can easily retrieve and/or submit it. Use abbreviations and acronyms judiciously, and spell them out the first time used. Excessive use of abbreviations and acronyms can impede assessors' understanding of the Written Commentary and could have a negative impact on your MOC decision.

Probing the Component 2 Prompts

The prompts are designed to: 1) provide relevant information to the assessor about how you applied your selected PGE to the lesson you planned and recorded; and 2) explain how your analysis and reflection of the lesson met the requirements of the component. You may address the prompts in any order, but the general recommendation is to respond in the order given, as this makes reading easier for the assessor. *Remove the prompts from the Written Commentary before submitting.* Notice that each prompt connects to one or more of the Five Core Propositions, one or more current National Board Standards, and/or the Architecture of Accomplished Teaching (AAT). Examples:

- How has your learning or professional growth, as described in the PGE, been applied in this lesson? (Propositions 2 and 5, AAT step 3)
- For the featured lesson, what were your goals, and how did they fit into the broader context of learning for these students? (Propositions 2 and 4, AAT step 2)
- Why is this instruction important for these students at this particular point in time? (Proposition 1, AAT step 2)
- How did you ensure fairness and equity of access and prompt appreciation of diversity among the students? (Proposition 1, AAT step 3)
- How does the video recording reflect your certificate-specific content knowledge? (Proposition 2, AAT step 2)

- Explain the impact of your teaching on student learning. Cite specific examples from the video recording and identify what they illustrate. (Propositions 3 and 4, AAT steps 4 and 5)
- Reflecting on the activity presented in the video, discuss any changes and/or additions that would have enhanced student learning. (Proposition 4, AAT step 5)
- Reflecting on the activity presented in the video, discuss any changes, additions, and/or next steps that would enhance your professional growth in the future. (Proposition 4, AAT steps 5 and 6)

COMPONENT 2 RESOURCES

Within the MOC Instructions are several resources to help you make decisions and compare your choices to the requirements of Component 2. Take the time to examine them thoroughly. There are lots of details on which to focus attention:

Page 21: Allowable Recording Time Frame
Pages 21–22: Video Recording: Editing and Audio Enhancement
Pages 22–23: Component 2 Specifications: Video Recording
Page 25: Component 2 Specifications for Written Materials
Page 27: Component 2 Checklist
Page 29: MOC Electronic Submission at a Glance
Pages 33–34: Appendix B: Recording Video Elements
Pages 35–38: Appendix C: Maintenance of Certification–Related Terms

WHAT WORKS!

Plan your Component 2 with the end in mind. Use the prompts and resources to know "where you're going," then use the destination as your road map for navigating Component 2.

Why These Work

Using these resources will give you access to all the information
and requirements needed to produce a complete, quality Component 2 video and Written Commentary.

Chapter Seven

Using Your MOC Instructions

WHAT YOU NEED TO KNOW

This book does not replace the NBPTS Maintenance of Certification Instructions!

The MOC Instructions document available on the National Board website (https://www.nbpts.org/wp-content/uploads/MOC_ Instructions.pdf) is your most valuable resource. In this book, I've presented the main requirements of each component along with interpretations, highlights, and tips, but the MOC Instructions contain much more. The instructions are the final word on all aspects of the MOC process and take precedence over any other directions presented elsewhere, including information on Facebook pages, what a Professional Learning Facilitator or other NBCT states or advises, and this book.

WHAT WORKS! What to Look For

The features listed below are spotlighted on many pages throughout the MOC Instructions. Each one gives pertinent information you need in order to submit your portfolio properly. Don't overlook these valuable aids.

- *Pay attention* to the gray boxes in the instructions. These contain vital information that will enlarge your understanding, provide a tip worth following, or give outline formatting requirements.
- *Hone in* on bullets. Bullet statements are crucial to your understanding of the requirements and make them easier to read.
- *Notice* bolded words and passages. They emphasize information of particular importance.
- *Utilize* diagrams, charts, tables, and/or checklists. They will help you plan, write, reflect, and revise your thinking, planning, and writing.

RESOURCES PROVIDE YOUR ROAD MAP

Each of the following features found in the MOC Instructions document will guide your thinking, planning, writing, decision making, and reflecting. They will quickly help you find information you need and provide answers to your questions.

Why These Work!

The MOC Instructions document contains all the information needed to generate and submit your MOC portfolio. Each gray box, each bulleted list, each chart or graphic carries significance and should be studied and followed. This book does not purport to cover every detail needed to successfully achieve MOC. Each NBCT is responsible for reading, understanding, and applying the instructions to his/her own portfolio submission.

Chapter Eight

National Board Writing

It's been a while since you wrote in the National Board "style," so let's review. The three "types" of writing—description, analysis, and reflection—are used to provide the most effective means of presenting clear, consistent, and convincing evidence. Writing your MOC application will have many similarities to the writing you did for your original certification or most recent renewal.

PRESENT YOUR CASE

Writing for the National Board is unlike any other kind of writing you've done since your original certification or renewal. Your score isn't determined by your grammar or sentence structure, fancy language, or the number of research citations you include. In fact, as you'll remember, some attributes of what is typically considered "good" writing don't apply here.

Writing for the MOC is, above all else, *evidentiary*, meaning written to present *evidence*. Your sole purpose is to present evidence of your accomplished teaching, learning, leadership, and collaboration. You must make a case for your continued accomplished professional growth the same way a lawyer argues a case in the courtroom—by presenting strong *evidence*. You are the defendant acting as your own attorney, presenting evidence of your professional growth since certifying or last renewing. Your Sample of Products (SOPs), video, and responses to the prompts are the evidence of your continued journey. The assessor is the judge and jury.

OVERVIEW OF THE NATIONAL BOARD WRITING STYLE

The two MOC components ask you to describe, analyze, and reflect on your teaching practice. You will:

- *Describe*—tell *what* happened in your educational setting;
- *Analyze*—tell *how, why*, or *in what way* a particular lesson was or was not successful teaching students;
- *Reflect*—look back at your practice to ascertain impact and possible next steps.

Just as an attorney uses a questioning style to elicit evidence, the National Board adopts a writing style that can be explained in three verbs: *describe, analyze,* and *reflect*. Each prompt connects to one or more of these to help you present information that is *clear, consistent,* and *convincing. Describe, analyze,* and *reflect* are verbs that tell what you must *do*. The noun forms *description, analysis,* and *reflection* are the *results* of your actions.

Description Tells "What"

When you describe something, you tell about it, you tell *what* occurred. You retell what happened in an educational setting. In court, a witness gives the facts in order to paint a clear picture of a situation. There should be no interpretation or judgment in descriptive writing. For the MOC components, you must respond with enough information for the assessor to form a picture or impression of what you want to depict. Key words in MOC Component 1 prompts that ask for description include *provide*, *describe*, *explain*, and *discuss*.

A descriptive passage:

- Tells or retells the main facts
- Is logically ordered
- Has enough detail to set the scene and give assessors a basic sense of the topic
- Contains accurate, precise enumeration where appropriate
- Allows an assessor to *see what you see*

Most teachers find description easy to write and typically tend to describe far too much. Although it is important to use description to give the facts and paint a picture of your PGEs, learning, and activities, it isn't the most important type of writing. Why? *It is the least evidentiary of the writing styles*. Description sets the tone, draws a picture, and gives the facts. But it doesn't deliver the most powerful dose of evidence. That is the task of analysis and reflection.

WHAT WORKS! Keep These Points in Mind When Describing

- Be succinct. Say enough to paint the picture, then *stop*.
- Decide which facts and details are significant and emphasize those.
- Concentrate on facts and details that show an impact on teaching or learning.
- Resist the urge to tell *everything*. Details matter, but don't go on and on.
- Follow suggested page limits.
- Support description with details and examples—but not too many.

Analysis Asks, "So What and Why, or In What Way?"

Description is the writing style that tells *what*. Analysis is the writing style that asks, *so what?* and *why?* Think of an attorney who puts forth a theory then goes about confirming or rejecting it depending on the evidence. Teachers make hundreds of decisions each day that are implicit in their knowledge of their students and content area, but they seldom need to express this minutiae orally or in writing. However, the analysis questions in each component require this intrinsic knowledge be put into words on paper. Analytical writing is important because:

- It is the most evidentiary of the three styles
- It demonstrates significance: *so what?* and *why?*
- It shows the assessor the reasons and motives (rationale) for your actions and decisions
- It interprets and justifies actions and decisions, backed up with evidence
- It shows the assessor the thought processes you used to reach decisions
- It examines why elements or events are described in certain ways
- It involves taking apart what occurred during the evolution of a PGE

   Prompts that ask for analysis may contain these key words: *how*, *why*, and *in what way*.

WHAT WORKS! Use These Sentence Starters for Analytical Responses

- Because I know _____, I (planned, provided, organized, taught . . .), which shows . . .
- I chose _____ because . . .
- There are several reasons why . . .
- The rationale behind my decision to _____ was . . .

- This was significant because . . .
- This impacted student learning by . . .
- Because _____, therefore . . .
- In order to _____, I . . .

The subject(s) being analyzed (PGEs, activities, SOPs, and/or video) must be available for the assessors. Clearly label your SOPs and/or video and refer to them in the text. Assessors will look at the SOPs and videos to compare them to the evidence in your prompt responses. Typically, the assessor reads your component, looks at the SOPs or video to see how they support your writing and "match up," and then reads the component again. The analysis helps the assessors see the significance of the evidence you submit.

Reflection Asks, "Now What?"

The descriptive style of writing tells *what*—like a witness giving testimony. The analytical style asks, *so what?* and *why?*, like an attorney questioning a witness or a scientist. The reflective style goes a step further and asks, *now what?* Reflection is like a jury looking back at the evidence to decide a case, or a follow-up visit to a doctor to monitor a course of treatment. Reflection is a kind of self-analysis that:

- Explains the thought processes used *after* implementing professional growth learning or a teaching experience
- Tells how you would make decisions in the future
- Is retrospective
- Explains the significance of a decision
- Indicates the impact of a decision, activity, or action
- Reviews instructional strategy choices
- Sets new goals based on your analytical conclusions
- Demonstrates your understanding of the National Board Standards

Prompts that require reflection ask you to look back at your PGEs and/or look ahead. Analysis and reflection often overlap. MOC reflective prompts ask you to reflect on:

- Ways your PGEs impacted student learning
- How changes, additions, or next steps might enhance your professional growth
- Patterns that might have emerged as a result of your professional growth

Reflection assumes that analysis has already taken place. A typical mistake candidates make is to retell, rather than reflect. When you reflect, you *explain* and *interpret* what happened, then tell what should come next. You look back, then forward. Use these pointers for reflection:

- *Be honest.* There is always something that can be done better. No lesson is perfect.
- *Show connections.* Keep reflections tightly connected to the PGE discussed.
- *Focus* on the impact your PGEs had on student learning.

WHAT WORKS! Use These Sentence Starters for Reflective Responses

- In the future I will . . .
- A key success was . . .
- An area for improvement is . . .
- My plan for next steps is . . .
- If I were to do this again . . .
- I learned _____, which will help me _____ next time by . . .
- Before implementing this PGE, my students _____, but because of this experience . . .
- Through this PGE I learned . . .

Why These Work

The boundaries between analysis and reflection are not always clear-cut. Analysis focuses on *so what?*, while reflection focuses on *now what?* Analysis is about the past; reflection is about using the past to determine future actions. Understanding reflection will make your writing stronger.

DANGER! STYLE FAUX PAS AND PITFALLS

While relearning to write using the National Board style, some writing hazards emerge. Watch out for these and avoid them. For example, read the following passage:

> The students were introduced to their new vocabulary by using flash cards. After practicing as a whole group, they were divided into study groups. First they were assigned jobs within the group. Each group was provided with a set of flash cards and a worksheet to reinforce their learning.

Question: What is wrong with the above passage? Answer: *The teacher is missing!* Nowhere in that passage is the teacher mentioned. Who is the teacher? Where is the teacher? When writing your components, you must put yourself in the picture—clearly, consistently, and convincingly. How do you do that? Fix it using *I statements*:

> *I* introduced students to their new vocabulary using flash cards. After practicing as a whole group, *I* divided students into study groups. First *I* assigned jobs within the group, then *I* provided a set of flash cards and a worksheet to reinforce their learning.

Look again at the rewritten passage with pronouns that put the teacher into the picture and with active voice verbs. Do you see the differences? *I* statements are the strongest writing construction you can use.

WHAT WORKS! Make Yourself Visible within Your Writing

Be careful with the pronoun *we*. It is stronger to say "the students and I," rather than "we." That way it's clear just who *we* are because *you* are in the picture. Use *we* sparingly. Use it once, then switch back to *I*.

- When using *we* to show collaboration, use it once, then turn the focus to your own contribution and switch to *I* or *my*: I collaborated with my department to plan the science fair. *We* each had assigned roles. *My* role was to . . .
- Use the active voice because it is clearer, more direct, and more concise. Sentences using passive voice are wordier, longer, and less clear than those using the active voice: *I* planned, *I* learned, *I* studied, *I* collaborated, *I* led, *I* organized, *I* wrote, *I* initiated, *I* worked.
- Use helping verbs and -ing endings sparingly. For example say: *I* provided _____ instead of _____ were provided . . . or I was providing. After writing a draft, go back and highlight each verb phrase with a helping verb and/or -ing. Then rewrite as many as possible in the active voice.

Why This Works

Passages are much stronger when the teacher is clearly in the picture, and active-voice verbs show who performed the actions expressed. There are also details to demonstrate how this teacher's actions support the National Board Standards.

MORE WRITING FAUX PAS AND PITFALLS

- Preaching from the pulpit: This occurs when a candidate uses the written commentary as a soapbox. Avoid inserting personal views and frustrations into the Written Commentary. It is a waste of words and space. Accomplished teachers are able to demonstrate professional growth and student learning in spite of difficulties and obstacles. Assessors score only *evidence* of the National Board Standards, so it is important to use words and space to demonstrate your evidence.

- The ESP communicator: When candidates don't explain their actions and decisions clearly, the assessor is left to connect the dots. Be careful not to assume that the reasons for choices are so obvious that no explanation is needed. Some candidates may be clear about what they *do*, but may write ambiguously or not at all about the thinking processes that led them to a particular decision. You must explain the thinking and decision-making processes you applied to your PGE choices, video, or other artifacts used in the MOC components. Never assume that an assessor will "see" evidence without an explanation. Explain your decisions and choices.
- The feelings guru: This candidate substitutes feelings for concrete evidence. Work to eliminate all *I believe, I feel, I tried*, and *I think* statements from your writing. Although teachers are very caring people, the National Board components are not the place to lay out your personal teaching philosophy or beliefs. Statements such as *I believe all children can learn . . .* or *I feel that all students should . . .* , however true, are irrelevant to the process. The assessor looks for *evidence* of a teacher's effectiveness, and a teacher's philosophy is not a measurable piece of evidence. Assessors look for evidence in the form of specific examples, descriptions, analysis, reflection, and artifacts such as SOPs and the video. Avoid these pitfalls by returning to the trial lawyer analogy. You must present evidence clearly, convincingly, and consistently to the assessors who are the judge and jury.
- *Jargon* is the specialized language, words, and terms used within a profession. Use it sparingly. Too much educational jargon gets

in the way of understanding. The best writing is plain, simple, easily understood language—the kind you use when you talk.

WHAT WORKS! Following the Three Cs

Clear: Never assume anything and explain everything.
Consistent: Goals, activities, collaboration, etc., must match up and be connected.
Convincing: Build a wall of evidence with examples.

Add more Cs:

Concise: Make your point and move on. Write short, to-the-point sentences.
Correct: Use correct grammar and punctuation so the assessor can focus on your content.
Concrete: Evidence needs to be specific, real, and measurable, not vague or ambiguous.

Why This Works

Clear, consistent, convincing writing showcases your evidence and provides sufficient evidence to maintain your certification.

WHAT WORKS! Strong Verbs, Strong Phrases, and *Bloom's Taxonomy*

Writing strong National Board components does not require a fancy vocabulary. The assessors come from all 50 states, big cities and small towns, and are teachers just like you. Ask yourself whether anyone, from anywhere, will understand what you wrote, and you'll be on the right track.

Strong verbs and phrases describe accomplished teaching actions and qualities that have meaning within the National Board Certification process. They are words that help you showcase your professional learning as described in your PGEs and the National Board Standards. They are, for the most part, plain, strong verbs and descriptive phrases. Using these verbs and phrases in your writing can lend clarity and strength to your descriptions, analyses, and reflections. But the criteria for using them are authenticity and honesty. They must have meaning within the context of your teaching practice. Here are some examples:

- Strong verbs: I encouraged, developed, designed, guided, supported, organized, facilitated, chose, chose to, selected, challenged, provided, gave, taught, engaged, demonstrated, learned, modeled, measured, asked, practiced, assigned, performed, contributed, impacted, influenced, instructed, questioned
- Strong phrases: students as risk-takers, ways of learning, learning community, lifelong learner, build self-esteem, promote student understanding, appropriate assessment, constructive feedback, fairness, equity, goal related, integrated learning, behavior intervention, high expectations, insightful questions, meaningful, learning goals, outcome-based, rich and in-depth, inclusion, productive classroom, cooperative groups, parent partnerships
- More strong phrases: community involvement, collaboration, diverse perspectives, beyond the classroom, high expectations, problem solving, real-world applications, rich variety of sources, student ownership, teacher as a learner, teaching strategies, unique learning needs, varied assessments, work collaboratively, standards-based, content-oriented, application, direct impact on student learning, I learned, I should have, now I understand, relevant characteristics, motivational

Bloom's Taxonomy is a useful reference for finding effective verbs that indicate levels of learning and for planning appropriate lessons. Here is a recap (from lowest to highest levels):

- Remembering: define, memorize, record, identify, label, list, locate, match, name, recall, spell, tell, state, underline, recognize, repeat

- Understanding: restate, discuss, describe, explain, express, identify, interpret, retell, review, paraphrase, put in order, summarize
- Applying: apply, conclude, construct, use, dramatize, illustrate, show, sketch, draw, give a new example, solve, operate, practice, translate
- Analyzing: distinguish, analyze, differentiate, appraise, experiment, compare, contrast, diagram, debate, categorize, classify, dissect, infer
- Evaluating: defend, judge, value, evaluate, support, argue, appraise
- Creating: assemble, construct, create, design, develop, formulate, write

Why These Work

These verbs provide evidence in your writing. They indicate your deliberate participation in the processes that make up professional growth and are examples of the language used in the Standards that shows evidence of accomplished teaching. Apply the litmus test to decide if something meets the criteria for being universally understood. There must be no confusion about the terms used in the written commentary. This is especially true for the names of programs or materials you or your school utilizes. Be sure to spell them out and give a brief explanation. Examples include the Individual Education Plan (IEP) and the National Council of Teachers of Mathematics (NCTM).

WHAT WORKS! Creating a Writing Framework

- *Make* the case that you are still an accomplished teacher by showing evidence of professional growth. You are the lawyer. The assessors are the judge and jury.
- *Connect* the three styles of writing—description, analysis, and reflection—to the prompts.

- *Keep* description to a minimum. Description tells *what.*
- Analysis asks *so what?* and *why?* and is the most evidentiary type of writing.
- Reflection asks *now what?* and is a type of self-analysis.
- *Provide* concrete examples of your actions and decisions.
- *Write* in the first person as much as possible.
- *Use* strong verbs and the active voice.
- *Avoid* using large amounts of educational jargon.
- *Be* authentic.

Why This Works

Your writing is the "legal brief" of your portfolio. It contains all the evidence to show the assessors that you are an accomplished teacher.

FINAL TIPS

- Limit bolding, underlining, and CAPS. A little goes a long way.
- Be as consistent as possible with verb tenses. Match the tense of the prompt.
- Talk *to* the assessor, not *at* the assessor. The assessor is your audience.
- Write in your own voice. Don't lose yourself in the writing process.
- State the *significance* of events.
- Spell out all acronyms the first time used.
- Streamline writing and cut the fluff. Edit! Edit! Edit numerous times!
- Avoid helping verbs and -ing forms of verbs wherever possible.

 Finally, be sure to:

- Back up your writing on your computer often!

- Pay attention to page limits. The assessors stop reading when they reach the stated limit.
- Follow portfolio instructions exactly.
- Answer all parts of every question/prompt. Respond *to* the question, not *about* it.
- Show impact on student learning.
- Connect your PGEs to the National Board Standards.
- Study the Architecture of Accomplished Teaching for insight into the prompts.
- Give up stressing about the vagueness of the prompts. It will only drive you crazy.
- Accept that there are many ways to address the prompts. The *right* way is with whatever information is true for you!

About the Author

Bobbie Faulkner spent 38 years teaching grades K–6 in Kentucky, Ohio, and Arizona. She is a Middle Childhood Generalist, Renewed. She has been a Candidate Support Provider for nearly two decades and has mentored hundreds of candidates in person, on Facebook pages, and through workshops and webinars. She has written previous *What Works!* books for candidates undergoing their first certification process.

9 781475 858501